Kenneth Leighton

Missa Sancti Petri

for SATB choir, with soprano, tenor and bass soloists, and organ

For the 750th anniversary of Peterborough Cathedral.

Commissioned by Peterborough Cathedral with funds made available by the Eastern Arts Association. First performance by the Choir of Peterborough Cathedral, conducted by Christopher Gower, on 4 October 1987.

Duration 15 minutes

EXCLUSIVELY
DISTRIBUTED BY

HAL LEONARD
CORPORATION

14021611

U.S. $12.95   NOV290692

nited
Suffolk IP33 3YB

ISBN 0-85360-853-9

9 780853 608530

MISSA SANCTI PETRI

KENNETH LEIGHTON
(1987)

KYRIE ELEISON

(* change of manual)

6

8

GLORIA IN EXCELSIS DEO

13

(* the chords audibly detatched)

Ped.

18

24

SANCTUS and BENEDICTUS

(* The priest may intone as indicated — or alternatively the first bar of the organ part may be used as introduction.)

Lord,   O   Lord   most high.

thee,   O   Lord   most high.

Lord   O   Lord   most high.

Lord,   O   Lord   most high.

ancora
più **f**

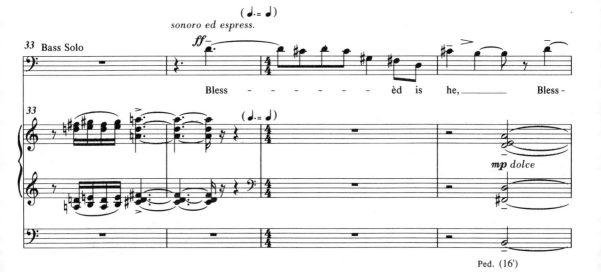

33 Bass Solo

sonoro ed espress.

Bless – – – – – – èd is he,   Bless -

mp dolce

Ped. (16')

AGNUS DEI

40

* Practice only

48

Published by Novello Publishing Limited
Music setting by Stave Origination

Edinburgh, March 1987

7/05(55502)
Printed in England